DID I MARRY THE WRONG PERSON?

DID I MARRY THE WRONG PERSON?

Gregory O. Chiadika, PhD, Fth

ISBN: 979-835-289-018-9

CONTENTS

INTRODUCTION

There are very few couple in our society today that have not made a remark similar to the title to this book – *"Did I marry the wrong person?"* either early or later in marriage, and I must candidly say that there are few today that are not making such statement, but are in between opinion. Once I had a fellow who was in his second marriage say – *"all I needed to do was to be more enduring and patient and understanding with my first wife"* some others in their second or third marriage will just tell you *"Am beginning to think the problem is me"* or *maybe I have bad luck"*.

In today's world some marriages don't last two weeks, am amazed at the rate of divorce suits in our courts while many others are just living together but has been turned to a "punching bag" or "cupboard" saying that she married the right person. What do you tell the man whose wife denies him sex for almost one year, or the man who is not allowed to have a say in his own home. How do you comfort a woman/man whose inner feelings and yearnings are not satisfied, people do say that no matter how long you walk on a wrong part it will never lead to the right part. What do we do, where do we go from here, how do we remedy the situation, can there be a remedy? In this book I will only attempt to render help, answer some questions that's in your heart, still some storms and calm the waves through the help of the Holy Spirit in Jesus Christ name. you may have to go over this book again and again, apply the principles as it relates to your peculiar situation. Your marriage can work; in many years as a marriage counsellor I have seen situations were two people that one may never match to be couples, lives a graceful and wonderful marriage. And I have seen where two wonderful, perfect as it were people, have terrible marriages and even divorce, so listen, open up your heart as you read, you will not regret it, in Jesus Christ name. Amen. The wrong person before you may just be one placed in your life so that you can be able to fulfil your purpose and destiny on earth. You know how salt can be harsh on the tongue but that small salt is needed to give the soup good taste on the taste bud of the tongue – what a contrast. Your worst enemy could just be or become your best friend.

CHAPTER ONE

IT'S EITHER GOD, THE DEVIL OR MY SPOUSE

"But the Lord God called to Adam, and said to him, where are you?

He said, I heard the sound of you (walking) in the garden, and in was afraid, because I was naked, and I hid myself.

And He said, who told you, you were naked? Have you eaten of the tree of which I commanded you that you should not eat?

And the man said, ***the woman*** whom you gave to be with me, she gave me (fruit) of the tree and I ate.

And the Lord God said to the woman, what is this you have done? And the woman said, ***the serpent*** beguiled (cheated, out witted, and deceived) me, and I ate". Genesis 3:9-13 Amplified Version.

What is marriage?

Marriage is the deepest and most intimate of all human relationships, a fusion of two distinct personalities into one.

The basic Greek word for "marry" or "marriage" is gameo, which literally means to "wed", "fuse together", "unable to give something up", "devoted", "Gameo" is derived from the same English word "gem" which means a precious stone or jewel. Now note that precious stones are hardly ever appreciated or cherished at the first glance, chemically, diamond is pure carbon (coal); coal that remains in the earth long enough for years under continuous heat and pressure eventually is transformed into diamond, and today diamond is the hardest and most precious substance on earth. Gold in its natural state is as dark as coal, you can rarely differentiate the two, but gold has to pass through heat (refinery fire) in other to shine and glow, it's the heat that purifies it. so the harder things get, the stronger the union grows; precious gems are rare, so is a genuine marriage.

Imagine Adam and Eve sited on sandy floor naked just receiving the fresh air from around them. They were simply enjoying the company, fellowship, presence of each other. They had no children but there was a lot talk about. Even their silence meant a lot of them, but in the moment of fellowship, Satan began his own conversation with Eve, aside the husband. Let me just say this here, whatever makes you so far from your spouse (even though you are still living together), is not from God, God does not join people in marriage to separate them, but to fuse them to become one.

Notice from the bible verse above that Adam and Eve although together in same location were busy doing their own thing; Adam properly focused on his activities and the things he would have to do next. He was properly appreciating nature, his environment. While Eve was yearning for someone to talk/discuss, chat with, someone to tell her feelings about life, their destiny and challenges. Adam did not see the devil as an enemy, even though he was close enough to hear all they were discussing. To him they were trivial issues; he had a more serious task which was to cultivate the garden before him. So when asked by God, what went wrong, he quickly exonerated himself and pointed the accusing finger at his wife "Eve" she gave me (fruit) of the tree and I ate". He further accused God of being the one who brought the problem "the woman you gave me" in other words, if He (God) had not given him (Adam) the woman there won't have an opportunity to fall. And that he told God that he ate because his wife gave him to eat and not because he was attracted to it nor did he want to eat it. Then here comes Eve with her hand lifted up and mouth wild open "..........*Satan cheated, deceived me and I ate"*. She did not realize that what made her eat was her eyes and appetite for "better" things other than that which was made available to them. She did not even say "let's hear what God has to say about it", ignorant of who she is and who God is to her, she did not point the attention of the enemy to the authority they were under.

Today this is repeated daily, the man is always too busy with that which he wants and feels is more important (work, money making, most times), to recognize the needs of his union and that of his spouse.

Can you imagine what would have happened if they had discussed the issue before making a move. What would have happened if Eve had asked for the husband's opinion about discussing with Satan, what would have happened if Adam had taken his stand since he was not deceived? What if he had just filled in for his wife's weakness? What if he had rebuked

Satan and commanded him to leave his wife and union?

What if he stopped his wife from accepting the devil's bait? One cannot rule out the fact that they were both sincere, but the fact is that they were sincerely wrong. Am sure God being all knowing and all seeing saw the devil negotiating with Eve, but you know, He (God) also knew Adam had all it takes to stop the devil, the ungodly communion that Satan was offering his wife, but he didn't. they were both self-centered. Remove selfishness from marriage and you will see victory in every home. Let's remember here that marriage is fusion not an individual display – it's not one-man show. If it's a one-man show, it's not a marriage. Covenants are never initiated without the full involvement of the other party, even our covenant relationship with Christ is ineffective without full participation (verbally and actively). You have to find a way to carry your spouse along. Stop pointing to the devil, yes I know it's the devil but the devil has no power except the one you permitted. ***"Whatever you permit on earth is permitted in heaven" Matt.13:20.***

The relationship with your spouse would not have been if you had not permitted it, in the same vain, the present state of your relationship only exist because you permitted it; wither because of the things you do or the things you did not do, either as a result of ignorance or stubbornness. God only offered Adam and Eve the opportunity to repent by asking them what happened, for He already knew, but they never did. Until this day, spouses still point accusing fingers at their spouse. Right now, I command the scale that covers your eyes open in Jesus name. Those who have a wonderful lasting second marriage are those who realize their mistakes ad change, which if they had done they would not have broken the initiate marriage. Who you really are will be manifested in your marriage. Your marriage will stretch you, its intention is to make a better, accommodating, realistic, loving, appreciative, innovative, and mature you. some husbands and wives are complete strangers to each other. The man does not know his wife neither had the wife ever taken time out to know or understand her husband. They just react based on the actions of the other. When on the journey to discover your spouse, please always let the topmost thing in your heart be discovering solutions to your problems and having a successful marriage not realizing how wrong your spouse has been or analysis how better your life would have been with someone else. Even though there are principles to be learnt and there are facts and methods to embrace, we must never forget the peculiarity of every union. No one can completely, totally resolve your marital conflicts and challenges without your help – not even God can help if you don't let Him. God has given you that privilege to hold the key to unlocking the success of your union. I have observed that most couples that refuse to the heled or counseled end up in divorce – Fusion does not take place without melting of each element involved.

If no man or woman is made for another, then there is nothing like marrying the wrong person. Show me your friends and I'll tell you who you are. Did you marry the wrong person? Well that question is left for you to answer, if your answer is I married the wrong person then believe me your union cannot arrive at its God given destination – sooner or later termination will take place. But if your statement is my marriage will work regardless of who I am married to, then my friend you will find help from the God who initiated the marriage idea. Go to God not with complains alone but with quest for solution. Fear of failure brings it to pass if your mind and heart is filled with fear, what you fear will come upon you while the hope for success brings it to pass no matter the hurdles – faith will see you through, your faith in God will attract heavenly intervention. You will find grace to help in your time of need. Only remember that grace only flows when you allow it to flow. It comes in a spur of the moment, the angel of covenant comes to stir the water of salvation in our marriage, right at the mist of the conflict, please, embrace it, cling to it and don't let go. It might be painful to the human nature to keep quiet when you have a thousand and one word to say. I know it's difficult not to react when someone doesn't seem to understand when you are so sure about the right things to do or say, I'll tell you one thing I know – Divine Intervention is always better solution than any human strength or wisdom can procure. Give grace a change to help.

CHAPTER TWO

MARRIED BUT LONELY

Many people have the idea that once they are married, they will automatically not be lonely again. For them getting married is the final antidote to loneliness. No sooner than they are married that they realize that it's not so. This realization can be heart breaking for those who cannot manage/overcome it, it becomes a good reason to go out and search for someone who can be the solution to their loneliness. Quickly they find someone else, who provides immediate but very temporary antidote. So excitedly they will tell you – "finally I've found my missing rib, the one I've been looking for he/she makes my world go round, I just cannot get enough of him/her".

You see often amongst middle age groups, the old, at times among the young, young but still lonely. For amongst the elderly, it maybe the loss of a loved one and dissatisfaction with those presently around them. In today's world frequent occurrence of loneliness is caused by certain factors.

Absence of companion/friend or friends

The oxford advanced learner's dictionary described being lonely as a state which one is sad because one has no friend or companion. If you are a lover of people like me, you always love it when you see friends and love ones, you naturally feel lonely when they are not around. I suffered it for a while, after marriage, some of my female friends just terminated or friendship, I was naively surprised, I thought there was no reason in the world why they should cut off from me – little did I know their intentions and some would not want to be misunderstood by my wife. You see we often expect too much from people and believe me, if you expect too much from people, you will easily get depressed and lonely – learn not to hold it against people when they do not do what you expect them to do. You will definitely miss some kind of fun you have with certain people; I mean people cannot be replaced. You will however be amazed that the person beside you, your spouse, will comfortably play a role in your life than all those people put together cannot play – you are lonely because you want to be. You must develop your personal relationship with yourself. Cultivate the habit of enjoying the company of yourself. Develop your private time. discover things that improve you, that gives you satisfactions, and do them. If I had occupied myself with all those friends I use to have as a single man, am sure I would not have been able to write the number of books I've written in just few years. As a married man, your time must be properly utilized for maximal output. Discover what gives you joy; for some people, it's a good comedy, if you are lonely, an option is to slot a comedy and watch, if its football, watch it – you definitely won't go to hell for watching football – "*An idle mind is the devils workshop",* however important to note that what you do when you are lonely matters a lot; many have been driven to deeper captivity and oppression of demonic spirits because of what they did at the time of loneliness; some go into illicit sexual relationship such as having sex with animals (dog, horse etc.), children let with them or neighbor's children. The case of a woman who said she had a boy of seven years old, that always visit her in her lonely home, she would make the boy have oral sex with her (fondle her breast and virginal with his tongue). While she would do the same to his penis). It may seem unimaginable but it's happening – that boy may never live a normal life, parents should be more careful with their children (both male and female children). I was in a hotel room last year and they needed to do clean up so I sat along the lobby. While sited I heard a loud noise of two people having sex, even the cleaners heard it too. this noise when on for a while that everyone at the lobby waited to see the people involved. Some felt they must be on drugs or just wild. When the two people came out, it was a boy of ten or twelve years and a matured woman who claimed to be his mother, I tried to alert the hotel officials but they only responded that all kinds of things happen in hotels; could it be ritualistic or is she simply using that child to satisfy her self – certainly not for her child although believe me, the resemblance was there. You cannot imagine what man us capable of doing in times of loneliness and depression. Other people indulge in pornography and masturbation, these are also terrible and very addictive. You may not be able to stop it on your won, you need help, because whether you know it or not such attracts demons into your life and home, they will pave way for greater problems in your homes – "you cannot fellowship with demons and expect God to be your companion no way. *"The man who wanders out of the way of understanding shall abide in the congregation of the spirits of the dead" Proverbs 21:16 Amplified Version.* So whatever you do should edify you, and bring out a better you. once you discover yourself, uniqueness and potentials, you will not likely be lonely in your marriage.

Depression

This also if unattended to can pave way for loneliness. Depression sets in unnoticed often times. Men depression differs from the women's; men can mask their depression with becoming workaholic, they just want to work, work, work, while the woman that is depressed is difficult to please, she nags and easily gets upset. Some just sit down and eat, eat. This mental health illness can be cured. First, you must realize that you are depressed, you feel lonely and urgently need friendship. I can never be your friend no matter how much I want to, if you do not see me as a friend. Stop being a 'cry baby' wake up to your challenge and see a bright future – remember, you are your greatest doctor after God. You must be resilient at your pursuit of lasting happiness; laugh more, be more optimistic, celebrate today, be thankful to God for the many mercies He allows our way, see what God has given so freely to you; fresh air, eyes to see, ears to here, hands to feel, feet's to move, count your many blessings money cannot buy and you will be amazed all that God has done, have a purposeful daily routine that will help you. Stop looking to your spouse to find fulfillment, look up to God, your spouse cannot be God, discover your inner beauty and that of your immediate environment. *"Anxiety in the heart of man causes depression, but a good world makes it glad" Proverbs 12:25 NKJV*. If you have no one talking good words to you, talk to yourself. Speak good words to yourself and see yourself glow. Don't confine yourself, at least you have family relations you can talk to, or else in the church you go to, make new friends. That takes us to the next reason why people are lonely.

Friendship and communication

You must learn how to make friends, from you the person you met at the grocery shop to a colleague at the office; see every opportunity to make friends, with the right kind of people. People who are secretive end up being lonely; after a while people just withdraw from them. After your wedding, you should at least trust a friend enough to share your new experiences with, start with the common topic – 'sex', just say it the way it is, don't wait for them to come, you can visit too, thank God for GSM mobile phones, call or send text, but please be sure that the person is not of the opposite sex. Relationship they say makes the world go round. Feel free with your spouse regardless of his/her age or financial status. If your husband is ten years or more older, as long as you are married, you should be able to discuss with him, and that my dear is not being disrespectful, even God talks with man, moreover, your husband is not God, perfect love drives fear.

Remember you share a common destiny. I used to think my mum and dad were age mates; the way they would sit down for hours and talk and talk about everything.

Some barriers to communication

1. **Defensiveness:** if your minds are busy thinking up an excuse or exception to what your spouse is saying. *"He who answers a matter before he hears the facts, it is folly and shame to him" Proverbs 18;13.*
2. **Personal Biases:** Some people prefer certain tones or phrases. My wife says at times that am not kind enough with my choice of words and that they are very conclusive. And there are certain things we feel should be this or that, some things we will not welcome another view. Well it's time to break down the walls.
3. **Different Listening Styles:** Lack of understanding or gender differences in

communication (listening and conversation) can create problems. Women use more verbal responses to encourage the talker like "mm-hmmm" and "yeah" just to indicate they are listening while a man will use it only when he agrees with what his wife is saying women want you to respond after they are through expression themselves.

4. **Physical Exhaustion:** Mental and physical fatigue makes it difficult to communicate effectively, you will do your relationship a lot of good to give the tired spouse time and space to react, better still avoid confrontational issues when the person is exhausted. You know what they say about the tired horse – stubborn and very unyielding.

5. **Selective Attention:** Screening and information being shared. Some people just blank off when they have concluded what their spouse wants to say or is

getting at – you may be wrong – assumption they say is the lowest form of intelligence. Learn to listen with a deliberate attempt to understand what your spouse is saying. There is a bonding that takes place with tolerance, you also begin to appreciate the beauty behind your genital peculiar rites. Women love details while men would rather go direct to the point. Women hardly forget an issue until conclusions have been reached.

6. **Inner Struggles:** For instance, low self-image, *'old women are uneasy when dry bones are mentioned'* you can continue to be pessimistic about life, don't jump to the conclusions that someone is trying to take advantage of you, always have it in mind that your spouse love's you, and much more you are God's favorite. You will have to accept yourself before people will embrace you, voice out a

positive thought to cancel out negative thoughts, speak to yourself on daily basis, and put yourselves in God's hand and stop watching out to see how someone else accessed you. Please let your spouse know your inner struggles.

7. **Falsehood:** When you communicate in your marriage, one person on earth you cannot afford to lie to is your spouse. When the truth is not told in marital relationship especially, it will soon lose its flavor, chemistry, magic and after a while you will be wondering where the magic has gone – loneliness sets in – you become detached from each other – that's why you have to always tell the truth.

Every lie creates a vacuum that only telling the truth can fill up again. Some couples may have to begin again telling each other, not the things he/she wants to hear, but the truth; simple, sincere, ugly, unattractive but the truth. The worst thing in every union is lying to each other. The story is told of a woman who felt she should not discuss her sexual feelings with her husband; fell in love with a pastor that came to town and was staying with them, her husband would go to work every day and come back late, tired, worn-out with weak erection if any. The husband was to naïve to know that women also want sex, he was too simple to allow another man take his place in his wife's life – every woman needs attention, affection and affirmation, some call it the three A's;

Attention:

Spending to listen to her, watch and express your observations.

Affection:

That tenderness that only a lover will give, warm embrace, kiss in the public, love text, calls at mid days, tender touches, a warm smile.

Affirmation:

That reassurance that she is still No 1, that reassurance that she is attractive to you and special.

The woman in the story was too secretive so shall I say proud to tell her husband she needed his affection, attention, romance and sex. A man of God I respect highly said he was in his study preparing for a major program when his wife came in and greeted him in a very suggestive feminine way, immediately he knew he had to satisfy her hear yearning – bible requires that your spouse consent to your abstinence, the consent has to be from her else, your prayers be hinder. This man of God said that day there were new breakthroughs, creative miracles and great healings like never before at the meetings – believe me it pays to obey God than offer sacrifices. Please let me advice, voice out your feelings to your spouse, no matter what they are, any other person is a stranger. In the story we are talking about previously the woman continued to the point that her husband would see the other man's sperm on her pants. I know it's sinful, ugly and terrible; but whatever you allow will come to you. Adam left Eve and today we have a fallen human race, the adulteress in Proverbs 7 said *"for my husband is not at home; he has gone on a long journey: he has taken a bag of money with him and will come home on the appointed day"*. If you are a traveling evangelist, please for God's sake travel with your spouse and not your female personal assistant, how in the world can you be leaving in different cities in different countries, believe me, at every stage relationship grows, either close or apart. Money, wealth, acquisitions can never replace you; he/she needs you and not just your wealth. The woman in the book of proverbs was used to living a lonely life – her husband always goes on a long journey, leaves her with wealth and loneliness – women are solution oriented, the only solution she though best was to engage in adultery while her husband was away as a cure to her loneliness, she is now addicted to it, with a demon am sure holding her captive, now she can't stay without it. why marry someone who is never there. She is now a prisoner of sin, drawn away by desire, on loneliness part. She will likely contact 'HIV' or any other blood or venereal disease and give it to her husband who was never there. Yes, I know that certain times work can take one outside home, that's ok but don't make a habit of it. The regular hosts of prostitutes at hotels are married men who came for brief work/seminars in another city. If you can control yourself, how about your spouse?

As we conclude this chapter you must be aware that the major cure to loneliness is the presence of God. Absence of God creates loneliness, presence of God upon a life fills up loneliness. If you do not know Jesus Christ as your Lord and Saviour you will have an emptiness that only Jesus Christ can fill. Open your heart now and invite Him into your heart. Say these *"Lord Jesus I confess that I am a sinner, I believe that you are the son of God that you died for my sins, this day I accept you as my Lord and Saviour, Holy Spirit, come into my heart right now give me a new heart in Jesus Christ name".*

I command every yoke of loneliness and sin to be destroyed and I ask that the Spirit of God will come into you right now Amen!

After now, you must locate a bible believing church close to you and join, give me a call or write me via E-mail. Now that you are saved you must take advantage of the fellowship you have with the Holy Spirit and use every time you are alone to be alone with God, once you cultivate that attitude you will wish you had more time, than just sit down and look into the air or watch some dirty cable channels. You will grow in this practice of fellowship with God, minutes to hours to days, to weeks and even months, you can never get tired of spending time with God and you know what I notice, it always seems so short, time simply take wings and fly – I remember the first time I spent a day in God's presence I did not know it was evening, when l looked up and saw everywhere dark, I got up and though it must have been an eclipse of the sun – it only seem like few minutes. Remember Moses spent forty days and went back again to spend another forty days – amazing how much God wants you nearer and nearer. Make the Holy Spirit your friend today and I tell you, you will never be lonely again. The issue is not who you married, the issue is who you are. The statement to make is not that you married the wrong person but that you have to become the right person. Take advantage of your peculiar challenge and ride on the wings of the Spirit of God. The presence of God upon your life will attract people to you, who would gladly spend their whole day with you.

CHAPTER THREE

CREATIVE COMPATIBILITY

Being a Christian, God fearing and being in love with your spouse are very important in marriage, but they do not carry automatic guarantee of marital success. In the book of Genesis in the bible, Adam and Eve had to realize that although they were one same person separate they were very different from each other. How do you continue to stay with the woman who cause you to fall short of God's glory and would not admit it? For the woman how would she stay with a man who barley refers to her as 'the woman you gave me' and accused her for their fall?

In creative compatibility, the first step is your ability to realize that you are different from your spouse. You must see the differences, identify them very carefully, then boldly accept them in good fate and begin to take positive steps to flow with it. Adam and Eve would have just said, 'God we are not compatible, please try out another rib from my other side; God would have suggested creating another Eve for Adam, but no, He knew they needed to develop compatibility. They got leafs and covered, began to relate more freely together. And you see them having sex. In chapter 4 verse 1 they would have gone their separate ways for God drone them out of the garden; but no, the situation brought them closer together. They didn't go to the lion or elephant or gorilla to see if they would be more compactable no, they recognized the co relationship and did not see an alternative. Those who run away with another for comfort had that option in their sub consciousness long before they took that decision. Every human being has the ability to create compatibility it's a natural ability.

Start by taking out time to do that one or two things that both of you love doing together. It may be sex, please go ahead and explore it, other things will follow. It may just be taking a walk, anything whatsoever. Then make it a more regular affair, God will open your eyes to see more. If there are none, God is able to create compatibility.

Like a new born baby that cries and cries for everything; when wet, hungry, uncomfortable, so newlyweds react violently towards any uncomfortable situation so just like the baby begins to learn that life is not all about her/him and that crying is not the only out, he/she then learns to communicate clearer and clearer as the day goes by. So compatibility strives better as we improve in our communication skills and understanding. Babies like music, and given attention. Find out what your spouse likes, one thing for sure everybody no matter how old loves attention- 'there is a baby in all of us'. The man is eager to educate, change his wife and forgets the fact that *'people don't want to know how you know how much you care'*.

The woman burdened by your desire to see change in her spouse uses words to express her disappointments and her expectation she must realize further that 'physical words don't change people', only God can change people.

Look away from what you see, if you are looking for faults you will find many. Become accommodative, make your spouse feel at home, loved and much more accepted in spite of their weaknesses. Adam never mentioned the issue of the fall to Eve, It's not necessary, why dwell on it. It's already an open sour why sprinkle salt.

If you are warm, lively, enjoyable and outgoing person, more of a sanguine but your spouse is more of the moody, self-centered, easily offended and suspicious, such person, more of a melancholy. All you need to do is flow with their strength, such person (melancholy) are gifted, creative, loyal and self-disciplined, then all you need to do is celebrate their strength.

Remember that you are not as discipline as them and vice versa. Compatibility is not trying to change your spouse or make them do only the things you want them to do. If you do, you will be killing the person and making him/her irrelevant in the union. God rarely joins two people that are alike – they will bore each other. I had a friend as a single young man that may have been a good wife, but when I realize that we were more like each other, I couldn't stand it; I like talking and being listened to, she also likes talking and being listened to. Imagine if we had married someone we have to learn how to listen. It would have been something else, but you know what today my wife talks too. She leant from me, she talks more freely and I had to learn her act of listening that is very helpful to me today in my counseling work. Am a very passionate person, am so filled with zeal and I want to run but I turn back and I see someone holding me to take it easy - she will have a good thought before taking an action carefully and more organized. This can be a problem you know, depending on how you handle it.

The root word is patience. The oxford advanced learner's dictionary describes patience to mean, the ability to accept delay, annoyance or suffering without complaining. The ability to keep doing something that requires a lot of effort. Any step towards compatibility without patience is a wasted effort. You will have to bear it without complaining when I newly married, my wife and I had several reasons to have problems and conflicts but we chose not to fight, its compromise they call it, I call it overcoming and living in victory. In the morning she would want a cup of tea and bread with butter, while I would prefer a plate of rice with chicken or any solid food. We talked it over, she said its more healthy to eat light in the morning, she was right, but I won the argument cause I was brought up to eat whatever you felt like eating, you cannot change an adult over night; so we agreed that I eat rice with meat/chicken while she takes her tea. With time she joined in the rice meal. However, years later we talked about it more intelligently and today, if am not fasting I drink tea for breakfast, and she also. You are compatible you just don't know it yet. "Love does not insist on his/her way" if you love a person you must give room in your heart to learn to let them be themselves. Everything cannot be just the way you want it. Initially, I could hardly accommodate feminine play and tickling that my wife wants to do with me; she would want to kiss me in the public, seat on my legs and watch the television or hold my hands while we walk on the road. I was the opposite, I found it so difficult to call her 'honey' our pet name in the public, or to do all of those things she wanted to do. But see how people can change. I even kissed her today inside the church compound. It was difficult to have my bath in the evening and brush my teeth but today I remind her to make sure she does them when she is very tired. My wife can stay in door for one year if she wants to but me, I just want to go out and visit. Well, today she has learnt to visit and I have learnt to stay at home at times. When we are both at home, she cooks and I taste the food to see if the taste is good. I encourage her to start a good thing that she wants to do (if it's good and God's will) and she encourages me to stay on what am doing (if it's God's will). She's a natural athlete and am not, but I love cheering athletes, so she runs and I cheer. No matter the difference, make it work for your good."...*all things work together for good for them that loves God*... my marriage is working not because I married a perfect person, she is far from it, it's working cause we have learnt to accommodate each other's flaws and celebrate our strength. "if your wife can't cook why make a mountain out of it, if you can cook, please cook and move on; there are no two couples that are the same. Stop comparing your union with your parents or any other couple for that matter. If you cannot work your way out of pain and move on, then you are not ready to be married. Those pains are the making process, have you ever seen a child that walks and runs without ever falling in life? No sir. Permit me to say this, get a magnifying lens and view your anus, tell me how clean it is, if you put your smallest finger into it and smell it – can you perceive any odor – some people don't clean well, so the odor is more but no matter how much you clean it, you will still perceive odor, marriage is like that, stop listening to ignorant people that tell you, your spouse is the obstacle, when you know for sure that he/she is not the problem. Even the wildest beasts can be tamed, if shown some love and affection. Affection and love opens up your creativity and remove the mark. Instincts and you begin to channel it towards your union, you will see great changes and transformation. The only constant thing in life is change, there might be something you are not doing right, take time out to discover what you are not doing, ask the spirit of God to open your eyes to see those things you should and should not do.

Also being around older couple help out, especially when you ask them how they were able to stay together for so long, "let the older women teach the young women how to love their husband".

All I will add that the younger men also need some teaching too. No one is actually too old to learn.

David and Michal

Disappointment of one spouse over another because the spouse doesn't live up to the other's expectations of what a husband/wife ought to be often causes trouble in the marriage relationship.

Michal was a beautiful young princess, daughter of King Saul, and David was a handsome and daring hero soon to become king! You can imagine some of their expectations of each other.

Michal's expectation of her husband was high, coming from a king's palace, she expected that her husband should display some degree of decency in her behavior especially in the public, although she loved him, she couldn't stand his makeup and unmannerly expression of affection toward God. She did not remember that David was a shepherd boy, young and full activity, a young man who has never learnt to express love and had experiences rejection by his brothers, even his father forgot he had him, when prophet came to anoint someone in his house. All David wanted was a warm embrace and welcome from his wife. Everybody wants acceptance from their spouse, else you can never have the best of them. Evidently, Michal did not have David's kind of spiritual experience and she had not completely forsaken the former kingdom to which she belonged, a kingdom God had rejected. Life had to be her way or nothing. No wonder all through the bible she is referred to as Saul's daughter some people remain single at heart even through married. If only she had welcomed him, embraced his God and ways, she would have enjoyed him better than any woman David ever had. God was so displease with her rejection that her womb was closed by heaven. Be careful not to despise your spouse, for that person was made uniquely different by God, if you do, you are mocking God, and friend believe me, God does not find it funny. Your parents have lived their lives, please live your and leave them alone. Embrace your spouse in spite of the different culture, background, make up or race, and the God of heaven will honor you in Jesus name Amen! You may have to learn to eat some new kind of food, soup and life style, it's called adjustment, remember you are no longer single but a fusion is taking place in your life and fusion doesn't come easy. It's easier with elements because you cannot hear their cry but believe me they do cry. However, if there is a risk on life, you may have to see a counselor urgently – life cannot be replaced.

CHAPTER FOUR

AM IN LOVE, BUT WITH SOMEONE ELSE

There are several stories about people who are in love with someone else other than their spouse. And the reasons for this varies from one thing to the other, depending on the prevailing situation; Am told a true life story of a husband who the wife begged him to employ (a sister from their local assemble). After much persuasion from his wife, he employed her, not knowing where she would fit into in the company, he made her his personal assistant, and since she could type very well, he gave her a desk close to his so that she could type all his letters and documents. They would work so late at times alone in the office for hours. One day his pen fell and he bent down to pick it from the floor, as he lifted his eyes from the pen on the floor he was looking straight into the young lady's underwear. Innocently she left her laps wild open, not knowing he would bend to pick his pen. He stared and stared until he was captivated. Nothing happened that day, only that she noticed that everything she requested for he granted her and even added extra. In her bit to show appreciation she would hug him and end her every sentence with 'thank you daddy'. He couldn't tell his wife about his feelings for his office assistant. They would stay late this time around just to talk and talk for longer hours the first time they hugged she made sure her two breast rested comfortably on his chest, he said it felt so good (she was young with firm breast) and he wanted more, it was as if he would die if he didn't feel her body and before they knew it, they had sex in the office, again and again – they both enjoyed it, even though they knew its wrong. His wife had not given him sex for three weeks, (she had been fasting and praying), and for the young lady 'stolen water is sweet', she can't remember when lasts she had sex. So the relationship started, and continued until they could no longer hide it. The man says he's in love with the lady and cannot stand his wife with four children. We have prayed and counseled but they said they are made for each other, the young lady is not sure how long it will last but she wants to enjoy every bit of it while it last. He gives her money in quantity that she had only dreamed of, her parents were happy and glad that God had sent a help for them. But how long will ill-gotten wealth last? They were just back from their trip (they had traveled to London) when the young lady feel ill, in initially pregnancy was suspected but the symptoms were not exactly pregnancy signs. They went to the hospital and several tests were run. It was discovered that she had AIDS, she was "HIV" positive, how: she remembered that before she resumed in that office she had a quick sex with her former boyfriend who just came visiting and had given her some money. The news of her illness spread fast, the whole office got to know, 'oga' her boss also went for a test but was negative. He did not believe it , but right there he repented and thanked God for having mercy on him, all the love he said he had for this young lady disappeared, he asked his wife for forgiveness and vowed never to be unfaithful. The wife is a well-informed, so she forgave him but she said they would not have unprotected sex for at least six months and test carried out again on 'HIV'. In the six months, he did not even go near her for sex he would just hold her and sleep off. They both entered a long fast for six months. For those six months their relationship was heaven on earth, the other lady died after three months this man said he could even count the number of times he thought of sex, but before now it was an every hour thought. After six months, he went back to do the HIV test. The night before he went,his wife made love with him, not willing anymore to live on earth without him, it was foolish but glorious. So together they walked into the hospital. They ran the test and the result was still negative, somehow we cannot explain it but the man is alive today after many years. The whole episode was very romantic, today they are now about to become grant parents, one of their daughters had gotten married and is pregnant - praise God. He lost a lot of money treating the young lady he had an affair with for those three months she lived, he lost his prestige and honor in his immediate environment, but thank God he is alive to tell the story. Not many people are not that lucky, some never live to tell the story, few questions to answer;

1. Was he actually in love with the young lady?
2. Could he have avoided the affair?
3. Did the wife in any way contribute to him having a relationship outside?

4. How do you break off a wrong relationship and how do you win back your spouse?

Was he in love?

It's important we understand the fact that sexual love can take place between any persons regardless of age, background, or any kind of barrier. Sexual love is that love that exist between a male and female. Sexual love is based on getting sex and romance, that's all. Your feelings and thoughts come to play a major role. When sexual love is not directed towards the one you are committed, covenanted to in marriage, it is called lust. Lust wants to take; if he truly loved her he would not have sex with her; when you see a woman and all you see is sex, you have a problem. Remember, your body does not belong to you. You have no right to sleep with another person other than your spouse. So any feelings that makes you violate the laws of God cannot be love, God is love and therefore love has to be pure to be love, in lust, you are afraid of being caught, in love you are glad and happy that you can even tell God about it. No child of God will pray – 'God help me to love this other woman more', so if you can't make that prayer and expect God to answer you, why call it love? Love is from God, lust is satanic. You feel clean and whole when you are in love but, you are dirty, guilty and feel far from God when you are in lust. When am having sex with my wife I speak tongues at times and most time I get revelations after the sex – its God originated that's why. But if you have ever found yourself in bed with another than your spouse you may enjoy it but the feeling of quilt will be there, when you stop feeling guilty as Christian know that you are cut off completely from God – Satan is totally in control of you, stop now and make a change. Wounds of infidelity are like wounds on a diabetic patient, difficult to heal.

Could he have avoided the affair?

Certainly, once you have identified that you are attracted to your personal assistant/ secretary or any person as a matter of fact, you would do yourself a great help to admit it. I cannot think of a more effective way to hurt your spouse than to have an affair. Many will tell you that rape is not as painful as discovering that your spouse is having an affair. You must then take further steps to avoid it. Make sure you are not in the same office with the person alone, and if you can, dictate the kind of cloths she wears, any decent lady will not wear a micro/mini skirt to the office. You may have to make moves to distance the frequency of your meeting; change jobs, change department, office, change your mobile phone number etc. you must stop further contact with the person. In some cases, you may not be diplomatic about it, especially when the other person has made his/her intention very loud and clear. If you can, tell your spouse, and please don't expect an automatic change, just do the right thing. When I travel for preaching engagement, I don't counsel women alone in my hotel room, not that I don't trust the women, am just trying to help myself and them. Why do you share secrets with another person other than your spouse don't you know that secrets bring people close, complain about your wife to a single lady who does not know the challenges of marriage, you are setting yourself up for a fall. Don't go near the river if you do not want to get wet.

"With her much justifying and enticing, argument she persuades him, with the allurements of her lips she lets him (to overcome his conscience and his fear) and forces him along.

Suddenly he yields and follows here reluctantly like an ox moving to the slaughter, as one in fetters to the correction, to be given to a fool, (or as a dog enticed by food to the muzzle).

Till a dart (of passion) pierces and inflames his vitals; then like a bird fluttering straight into the net he hastens, not knowing that it will cost his life. Listen to me now therefore, o you sons and be attentive to the words of my mouth. Let not your heart incline toward her ways, do not stay into her paths for she has cast down many wounded, indeed, all her slain are a mighty host. Her house is the way of Sheol (Hades, the place of the dead) going down to the chambers of death. *Proverbs 7:21-27.*

If you have already fallen don't stay in it, rise now and walk away. In fact if you can run, fly, please do. When the same thought comes into your mind more than once about a particular person then you have to do something about it or else.

Did the wife contribute to his having relationship?

Again one would say yes, why bring another lady that you don't know very well to become your husband's personal assistant, it would have been better if he had gone on her own without your recommendation, your spouse will naturally treat someone you recommend special – if you must, let it be someone you are sure about for some people they must be careful about the kind of maid, lesson teacher, cook etc. they allow into the house and in few cases drivers. Then what in the world would make you deny your husband sex for three weeks. The man might have even said its ok and then he can stay away, when you must ask yourself is; before your intention to fast and pray, how often do you have sex in a week; then if you eat after the fast, why can't you have sex? See more on this on this in my book **"marriage without tears".** There are some tears we don't have to cry, by using common sense. However, I will say that there is no good excuse for infidelity. If a man's wife is not meeting his sexual need, finding another sex partner is the cruelest solution of all. If a woman's husband does not meet her needs for affection, she has no right to develop a romantic relationship with another man, you can talk things over; get someone who can effectively reach spouse, maybe her mother/father or pastor. You might both have to see counselor and that's one good step to take. When we were newly marriage we had a friend who said her husband rarely demanded sex, and my wife wanted me to take a clue from it but I refused, year later we discovered he had chains of undergraduate girlfriends he makes love to regularly.

How to break off from a wrong relationship

The journey begins by realizing how bad it makes God feel. Infidelity is first an act of insult to God, who initiated marriage. Tell God you are sorry and make sure you mean it, remember He see the heart.

When you have told your spouse, please don't expect an embrace, she would be very angry and will show it, especially if it's your first time. You will have to bear with the anger burst and rage. Don't defend yourself, just apologize.

You may need to recite your marital vows again together and pledge your commitment, where possible before a servant of God.

If you know what will make her happy, please do it, show some love, become more tender and just let her talk.

Spend more time together alone with her, maybe you would have to go out to a quiet place and just show affection and care to her. It may take time but the wounds will heal.

Spend time to pray, not only for yourself but also for your spouse, for God's grace to overcome the pain. Remember that forgiveness is a decision but trust is a process. You will have to build trust. Start by doing honest, tell her at the right time the things you cannot bear, things you dislike, be sincere and open. If you prefer her cleaner tell her, if you do not enjoy your sex life, oh please tell your spouse work on improving your married life. Make your spouse your best friend and learn to appreciate the little things he/she does. You are not allowed to keep secrets, share even your thoughts, remember the two shall become one flesh. Where you do not agree, you can agree to disagree. Let your spouse know your feelings about every matter. Its things that we trivialize that later become major issues. The greatest gift you gave to each other is that you are naked and not ashamed. The loving feelings will naturally find their way back into your spouse heart as you trust God in faith. I once knew a man who was deeply involved with another woman, and his comments about it, is that he wish he would reverse things that he never needed to fall. And that although his wife has forgiven him, the memory of his unfaithfulness hunts him.

You must forgive yourself; see yourself as a new man. Your spouse may not see that you are a new man immediately you know how women can be too practical at times, it's ok, just make sure you forgive yourself and more on let the past stay in the past.

CHAPTER FIVE

YOUR EYES, HIS EYES

All through the Holy Scripture we see a lot of reference to the eyes, from the Old Testament down to the New Testament. This morning am woken by the Lord with thoughts on the eyes, and wondering what this has to do with the book am writing. My heart is enlightened on this revealing truth, basically put, the eyes enable man to see, your sight is dependent on your eyes, if you have bad eyes, then you will likely have bad sight. I might be standing before you, but if you cannot see me I might be making fun of you and you will not know it, you might feel my presence, (that is if you have developed your other senses effectively) but you cannot see me without your eyes. If a person does not have eyes, he/she is said to be handicapped, there are certain things you cannot do for yourself the eyes no doubt is important to the human comfort and completeness on earth. Some years back, someone brought a business opportunity to me in which within days I would obviously be rich. The only thing in it was that certain people would be cheated and I looked at it and simply said no to the offer. Unknown to me, I was being set up for a fraud, am so glad I said no.

One night my wife fell critically ill, we did not know what to do, earlier that day I had been tempted to compromise and had said no to it, you know the devil is a good planner, sets you up for a major fall but praise God, we have the master planner on our side whose ways will always triumph over all satanic plot. I held her (my wife – Uchenna) and simply called on the name of Jesus and she became instantly well. She later said while I held her, she saw Jesus walk into the room and touched her. You will trade your victory to sin. Your ability to see beyond now, seeing with the eyes of God, in this book practical steps and learning's that will keep you victorious regardless of already attained triumphs. Looking at today's world you would almost ask 'is it possible to stay holy' the obvious answer is yes. We shall discuss practical steps and ways to living a holy life, in a contemporary world. This generation is not the first to pose this question before God, and I will not promise you that it will be the last, but from generation to generation the answer remains the same – yes, you can stay holy. Wisdom is strength, understanding empowers from the inside out. You will be empowered from the inside out as you read in Jesus name.

The sight is a gift from God *"the hearing ear and the Seeing Eye, the Lord has made both of them" Proverbs 20:12*

Further, God gave specific instructions about the eyes.

"The light in the eyes (of him whose heart is joyful) rejoices the heart of others, and good news nourishes the bones" Proverb 15:30

So when you say or wonder if you have married the wrong person, its important to find out from whose eyes you are looking through, are you seeing things from your own perspective or from the perspective of God.

"don't think the way you think. The way you work isn't the way God's decree. "for as the sky sours high above earth, so the way I work surpasses the way you work, and the way I think is beyond the way you think".

Isaiah 35:8-9 (message translation)

The way the system of the world operates is entirely different from the way God's system operates. For instance; God's system says you call those things that be not as though they are, but the world says – 'what you see is what you get' they are both correct in a sense, only that you will have to ask yourself; only that you will have to ask yourself 'from whose eyes are you seeing from, yours the world's or God's.

Looking at Mary Magdalene, a woman who seven evil spirits had been cast out from, one may quickly say that she was qualified to rob the feet of Jesus with oil more so in public? Any pastor that does that day has ended his ministry by himself critics will crucify him. Jesus saw beyond her past and saw God's eyes, a repented Saint and a work in progress. do you know that she later became one of Jesus close Ministers even unto death?

"And many women were there beholding afar off, which followed Jesus from Galilee, MINISTERING UNTO HIM" Matthew 27:55

Things are not always the way they appear, always remember, 'things change situations and people can change also. Often, people's behavioral pattern is molded by the environment they grew and past experience they have had. A rape victim cannot just open up herself to any man, even if it's someone she is married to, she is cautious and unnecessarily hostile and rigid. It takes a man of faith to be patient and call froth those things he not seeing as if they are existing. It's a personal decision to work by faith and not by sight. Seeing Jesus allow Mary Magdalene rob his feet most have alarming for some of the apostles and disciples of Jesus but Jesus could see her heart.

Question; do you look deep enough to see the heart of your spouse, understand their pain, acknowledge their weaknesses and still celebrate them regardless?

Jumping into taking the decision to leave, ask yourself, if the tables was turned around, what would you want done to you? Relationship strive not because the guilty is punished but because the innocent is merciful. We all have our cross to carry, Apostle Paul says it even better *"And why do you think I keep risking my neck in this dangerous work?* I look death in the face practically every day I live. Do you think I'd do this if I wasn't convinced of your resurrection and mine as guaranteed by the resurrected Messiah Jesus? Do you think I was just trying to act heroic when I fought the wild beasts at Ephesus, hoping it wouldn't be the end of me?

Not on your life! It's resurrection, resurrection, always resurrection, that undergirds what I do and say, the way I live. If there's no resurrection, "we eat, we drink, the next day we die", and that's all there is to it. but don't fool yourselves. Don't let yourselves be poisoned by this anti-resurrection loose talk "Bad company ruins good manners". Think straight. Awaken to the holiness of life no more playing fast and loose with resurrection facts; ignorance of God is a luxury you can't afford in times like these. Aren't you embarrassed that you've let this kind of things go on as long as you have? 1 Corinthians 15: 30-33 (Message translation).

So look, but with the eyes of God. Allow his ways and thoughts to influence your decisions and imaginations. Don't depend on the story acted out by Hollywood or Nollywood or in fact by any wood. You just have to pave your own path through the eyes of God which is His word.

Email me at anointedabundance2005@gmail.com or call ±2348066241512 any time.

www.ingramcontent.com/pod-product-compliance
Lightning Source LLC
LaVergne TN
LVHW041235150826
845673LV00008B/2389

* 9 7 9 8 3 5 2 8 9 0 1 8 9 *